AF426365

I am smart.

I am strong.

I am right.

I am wrong.

I am quiet.

I am loud.

I am loved.

I am proud.

I am not perfect.

But I smile.

I am handsome/beautiful.

I have style.

I have feelings.

I cry tears.

I have courage.

I have fears.

I will lose.

I will win.
REPORT CARD
A
B
A
A
A

I'll help out.

I'll make friends.

I'll have fun.

I will learn.

I will twist.

I will turn.

I'll be here.

I'll be there.

I'll use my words.

I'll use my ears.

I will change.

I will grow.

I will go far.

Don't you know?

I'll keep trying.

I have dreams.

I'll never give up.

I'll do all things.

I am special.

I am me.

I am important.
You Matter
Shine Bright
Be Kind

I will always be.

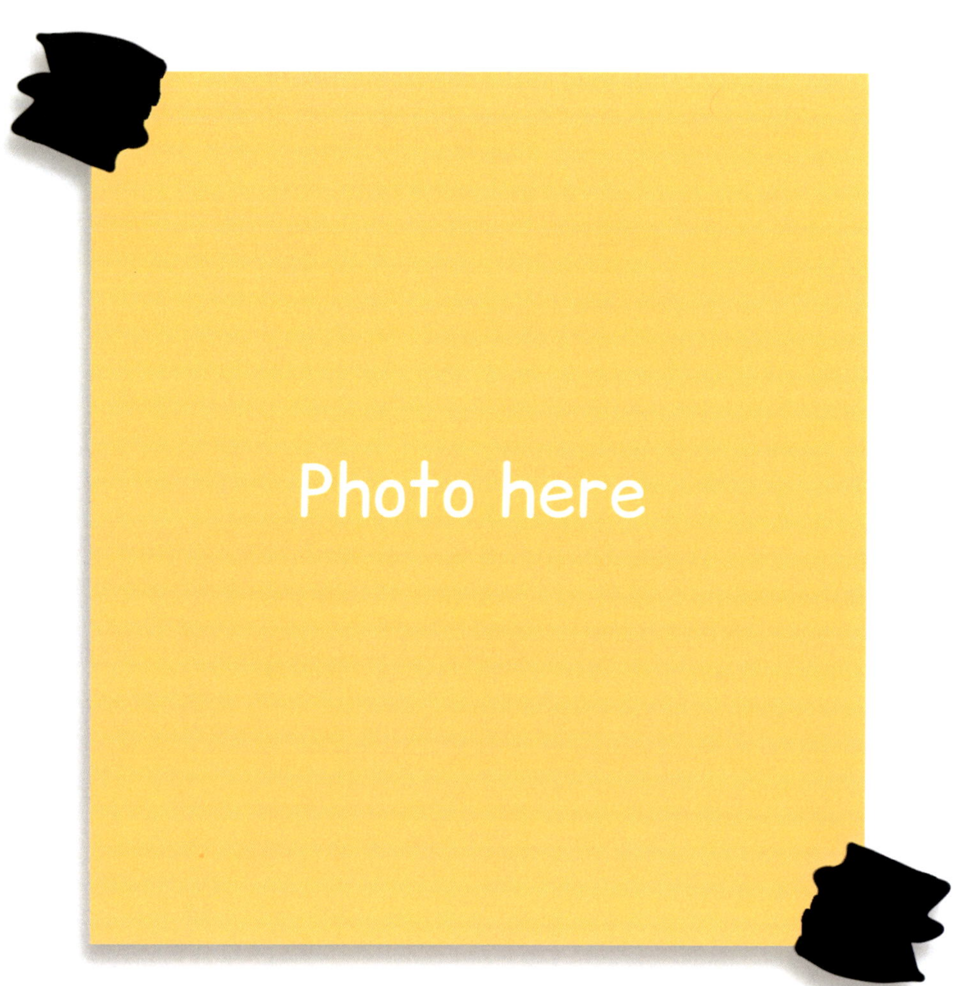

"I AM _____________

& I LOVE ME."